Pieces of a Puzzle

PIECES OF A PUZZLE

WRITTEN BY: HOWARD C. PERKINS III

WITH: HEDDRICK MCBRIDE

ILLUSTRATED BY: HH-PAX

EDITED BY: JILL MCKELLAN

Pieces of a Puzzle

Copyright © 2018 McBride Collection of Stories

All rights reserved.

ISBN: 198667634X

ISBN-13:978-1986676342

DEDICATION

This book is dedicated to every parent, family member, teacher, tutor, therapist, nurse, and doctor who has ever had the joy of working with and helping these wonderful children on the Autism Spectrum. It is your tireless and often unsung efforts to facilitate breakthroughs that inspire me. To the students I have taught at The Forbush School at Glyndon, The Children's Guild, and City Neighbors High School, you have left an undeniable mark on my life and my heart.

To the Graduate School of Special Education, at Coppin State University, Dr. Hattie Washington, Dr. Daniel Joseph, and Dr. Taylor, you all have given me the confidence and drive to never stop learning or teaching.

To my awesome mother, Valerie Perkins-Lee, I am honored to be able to carry on your dream of being a Special Educator. To my wonderful children Layla and Darien, my love for you is limitless. Continue to grow and keep God and education first in your lives.

Pieces of a Puzzle

Always chase your dreams. Thank you Tyra for listening to my ideas.

Thank you to all my brothers of Iota Phi Theta Fraternity, Inc., building a tradition.

To Kennard, Tracy, Nikki, and Vernon, you are all example of spectacular parents.

To Heddrick, thank you for seeing my vision. See you on #2.

I want to send a very special thank you to Autism Speaks for the supporting these wonderful families.

Howard C Perkins III

Pieces of a Puzzle

Pieces of a Puzzle

My Name is Taylor and I am 7 years old. I have Autism. I am non-verbal, which means I have not talked yet. It's not that I don't want to talk; I just don't know how to get the words out yet. I like to read and hug my teddy bear, Mr. Fuzzy. My mommy always says she knows that I will talk soon and she helps me every day. I think I'll talk soon, too!

Pieces of a Puzzle

Pieces of a Puzzle

Ms. Davis's 2nd Grade class is always lively and fun. Kids laughing and clapping is how learning is done. The room is full of energy as all the students gather in groups at different stations to play. All but Taylor—she sits alone most days. It's just Fuzzy and Taylor, the best of friends, and she looks at him and wishes she could tell him but that's where the hard part begins. The thing about Taylor is she has never spoken a word.

From off in the distance, Ms. Davis calls out. "Taylor, is there anything you want or need?"

Pieces of a Puzzle

Taylor just flails her arms, and continues to read. What is amazing is Taylor reads big kid books and does really hard math. She can't get her words out but it's pretty neat that she can manage a laugh.

The day goes on and Taylor's mom comes to pick her up. Marie, Taylor's mom, comes and gives her a big hug.

"Good afternoon, Ms. Davis, how are you?"

"I'm doing well and how is everything with you? We are very excited for when Taylor will start to speak."

"We work on it every day. I repeat her sounds and talk to her lots, leaving time for her to try and talk. She holds my face to feel my mouth move."

"That's wonderful! I know she will talk, it's going to happen soon."

Pieces of a Puzzle

Pieces of a Puzzle

"Okay honey, let's try this again. When there is something you want you say, 'I—WANT—THAT.'" Taylor just waved her arms like she was swinging a bat. "No sweetheart, say 'I—WANT—THAT.'" It's almost a game that the two play as Taylor watches her mom's mouth and watches her face. But she always tries to do it and wants to talk. "Taylor, come on sweetie," her mom encourages. Sometimes she moves her arms and other times she might decide to kick her feet. Mom keeps asking questions slowly and trying to get her to speak. "Is this what you do when you want to eat?"

"Tell me what I should do so we can make the words come out of you. Maybe I should tickle you and the words will come out, even if it's only a few." Taylor will hold her arms out sometimes and her mouth forms to say a word but still, no matter how hard she's tried, nothing comes out.

Pieces of a Puzzle

Pieces of a Puzzle

The next day, when Taylor's mom woke up, she found Taylor in the kitchen, trying to get cereal from the cabinet.

"What are you doing? Do you need me to grab it?"

Taylor hits the counter because she's upset.

"Mommy can get you whatever you need me to get."

Taylor starts to cry, looking around for Mr. Fuzzy. He might make her feel better.

Her mother says that when she's ready to say something, she can tell her.

Pieces of a Puzzle

Pieces of a Puzzle

Hola', my name is Gabriella and I am 5 years old. I am autistic, as well. I love to play with dolls and blocks. Sometimes I do things because they feel right, but mi' Madre y Padre' says I shouldn't do some things. I don't know why all the time. I am still learning this stuff; it's new to me.

Pieces of a Puzzle

Pieces of a Puzzle

Gabriela started playing with her blocks, stacking them up to the ceiling. She didn't want to stop.

"My, my," Madre said, "you sure have stacked a lot."

Then Gabby knocked them over with a mighty chop.

"Why did you do that?" Madre asked with care.

"I don't know, just because they were there."

"You can't do everything that you feel like doing without a care."

Gabby didn't know why she always did what she did. Sometimes a feeling just showed up inside of her and she couldn't get it out of her head. She would just do it. You know how when you see something you don't like and you just want to move it.

Pieces of a Puzzle

Pieces of a Puzzle

"Gabby, do you know what boundaries are?" Madre asked.

Gabby shook her head no and started to walk away.

"Boundaries are used so something does not go too far. You have to respect people's things and other people's space. You do that by not moving their stuff or getting in their face."

Gabby thought about what Madre said and gave her reply. "I know I can do that, I promise I can and I promise I'll try."

"It'll be easier if you remember that you can't change things without other's permission."

"Okay, Madre, I think I have it now. If it does not belong to me I should put it down."

Pieces of a Puzzle

"These are things we all should do, but you learned today to think of other people when you want to play. When your body wants to do something that you're not sure is right take a minute to think about it. Then you will get it right."

Pieces of a Puzzle

Pieces of a Puzzle

My name is Justin and I am 9 years old. When I was 2 years old my parents were told that I have an autistic spectrum disorder. I'm not *that* different from any other kid. I do very well in school and I listen to my parents. There are a few things that do make me different. For example, big crowds make me nervous. One thing I really like is dinosaurs—I mean a lot, a whole lot! And sometimes I have difficulty making friends but I love everyone.

Pieces of a Puzzle

It was the end of the school day on a sunny afternoon. Justin was standing on the steps and his mood was blue. He's usually one of the happiest kids ever but he could not find his smile. Things weren't great for him, a very unique 3rd grader, that day and he wanted to talk to his big sister when he got home.

Pieces of a Puzzle

Pieces of a Puzzle

"Stephanie, where are you? Are you here? I need to talk." He called out her name and started to walk. There was no answer; his nerves made him antsy. Stephanie shouted out, "Boo!" She jumped from the pantry.

"What are you doing, trying to send me to the hospital?"

"Well it's my job as your big sis to scare you as much as possible."

"Okay, so I have a question. Do I look like an octopus or any kind of monster? Tell me truth, I really want to know."

"You don't have eight arms so I would say no."

Stephanie looked at Justin and was very curious. "Why would you ask that anyway?"

"Because you have friends and I'm having trouble making any. I just need to know, how do I get them?"

Pieces of a Puzzle

Pieces of a Puzzle

"Hi Mom, I felt really sad today."

"Tell me why you have the frown on your face."

"I looked around at recess and didn't have anyone to play with. I have a big question and I need to know, how do you make friends so you don't have to play alone?"

"Don't worry, son, I think I can help. I have a plan."

Justin's dad comes in. "What's wrong with the little guy? Looks like he had a rough day. You can see it in his eyes."

Mom smiled sweetly. "This sometimes happens with Autism, his doctor said it could. Are you ready to use that plan we have just in case it would?"

The dad smiled. "It's family time and I will call Steph into the room. Some family time is what we need. It's definitely true."

Pieces of a Puzzle

Pieces of a Puzzle

Mom clapped her hands softly and began to speak. "This is the friendship game to help you make friends. We will ask a few questions before it all ends."

Justin shook his head, not sure what to think. "Do you really think this will help me?"

Dad patted his shoulder. "Son, relax it will work."

"Okay, I'm ready I guess it can't hurt."

"If I sit next to you in the lunchroom what do you do?"

Pieces of a Puzzle

"I say 'hi,' and then ask if I can share my lunch with you."

"Saying hello is fine but be careful about sharing your food, this new friend might only want lunch from you."

"Okay, whose next? You know I really love to learn."

"Let's try this one," Mom began. "You come out to play at recess and see a basketball game under way. What do you say?"

He didn't waste a moment to say, "I would say, 'I want to play.'"

"That isn't the way to say what you want or to talk to someone you want to know."

Justin sighed. "You told me to always be honest. I'm no good at this, Dad."

"We'll keep trying and it'll help you grow."

Pieces of a Puzzle

With the next card out, Steph took a turn. "This is my friend Kelly and we would like to play a game with you, what do you do?"

"I would give you and Kelly a big hug and let my happiness show."

"It's okay to hug me because I'm your sister, but when you meet Kelly for the first time you are better off shaking her hand or just saying 'hello.'"

"So, if I do all of these things I will have friends?"

"I know it'll work for you but the best thing you can do is just be yourself and remember that is how you make the most special friends."

Pieces of a Puzzle

Pieces of a Puzzle

Hi, we are Dai and Alexia, we are best friends. We both have autism. We go to the same school and we are also in the same class; we like to laugh and have fun. Sometimes our teacher says we are in our own world. Just a few years ago our doctors said we had to learn to use our imagination but we didn't know what that was. Now we do!

Pieces of a Puzzle

Pieces of a Puzzle

Dai and Alexi are best friends. When they play together their adventures never end. Alexi often things she is the queen in a castle. Then she imagines Dai fighting dragons without any hassle.

One day, not too long ago, Dai's Dad and Alexia's Dad took them to the park. They hoped they would play and it would make their imaginations spark.

Both kids had trouble playing alone; Austic kids sometimes go through that.

Pieces of a Puzzle

Pieces of a Puzzle

"STOP! Freeze!" Dai called out.

"We're coming to get the bad guys," Alexia added.

The two had so much fun pretending to be police officers and getting the crooks, they were always ready.

They got their ideas from cartoons and what they've read in books. Those were places to get great ideas for their imaginations to soar.

Dai described it quite clearly, saying, "Our dads' say when we play we are in our own world."

Alexia nods her head and smiles big. "That's because it's so much fun we can go where ever we want and be anyone or anything we want to be."

Dai added, "Yeah, like a teacher or a doctor, maybe even a tree."

Pieces of a Puzzle

Pieces of a Puzzle

Dai taps his chin and says, "I have an idea. Why don't we pretend to fly and be superheroes, jumping over buildings ten feet tall?"

"That would be great," Alexia eagerly agrees, "we can look for bad guys in there secret hideout, it'll be easy because we can see through walls."

Dai leaps and jumps and he starts to fly. Alexia runs like the wind as the world passes them by.

When you have Autism sometimes things are hard but having a best friend makes everything better.

Alexia and Dai realize how lucky they are, laughing at everything and making lots of silly faces, and even running in races.

39

Pieces of a Puzzle

Pieces of a Puzzle

When you have Autism sometimes things are hard but having a best friend makes everything better.

Alexia and Dai realize how lucky they are, laughing at everything and making lots of silly faces, and even running in races.

Dai looks at Alexia and a big smile spreads across his face. "When we are in our own world there is no better place."

Alexia agrees and adds her own thoughts. "We can imagine anything from a boat on the sea to a rocket in space."

They give each other a high five, agreeing that their world is awesome thanks to the other. Having a best friend with a great imagination is something they treasure.

Pieces of a Puzzle

Visit www.mcbridestories.com for more titles.

Pieces of a Puzzle

Made in the
USA
Middletown, DE

76078465R00027